THE IPHONE 12 PRO PHOTOGRAPHY USER GUIDE

YOUR GUIDE FOR SMARTPHONE PHOTOGRAPHY FOR TAKING PICTURES LIKE A PRO EVEN AS A BEGINNER

WENDY HILLS

You are welcome to join the Fan's Corner, here

The iPhone 12 Pro Photography User Guide

Your Guide for Smartphone Photography for Taking Pictures like a Pro Even as a Beginner

Wendy Hills

Disclaimer

Contents to Expect

About this Book for the Audience

This book will help you as a guide from a beginner to advanced level for anyone who was using an iPhone and switched to its newly introduced variant or migrating from other available devices to apple's iPhone, specifically iPhone 12 Pro. It will provide you with the most accurate information in a way that is simple and easy to understand.

Also, if you're not tech-savvy, but love photography and want to learn the basic and advanced use of the iPhone 12 Pro camera, this Guide is for you. For lovers of social media, Vlogging, capturing and recording special moments, this is a book you will love to read, it also includes some of the most amazing and cool tips and tricks to use the hidden features. It will serve as a permanent guide for your photography endeavor.

This book will do all it can to take away the rigors of researching how to perform various tasks on your new iPhone. It will also offer you a complete range of tips and tricks, hidden features overview and uses, from some of the most basic to more advanced features as a sort of knowledge base. So, if you an experienced iPhone user or a newbie, you will indeed find useful information related to iPhone photography and will be grateful you got your hands on this book.

If you or your friend is either switching to or buying an iPhone 12 Pro for the first time because of its amazing camera features and want to learn how to take great photos with a beast in hand, this is the book you should be recommending to him/her or buying for yourself.

Brand Statement

We will use this book as a fantastic user guide to help anyone who has purchased or wishes to purchase the iPhone 12 Pro phones. You will learn all about how to use your newly acquired iPhone 12 Pro for taking great pictures so that you can make the most out of your iPhone, either in social life, family use, or business life.

Introduction

Switching from an Android phone to an iPhone comes with its share of challenges and, not surprisingly, many people find that it takes them some time to adjust to their new iPhones.

For persons with love and passion for smartphone photography, having an iPhone becomes something more than just having a device for making and receiving calls but something that serves as a personal organizer.

Beyond that, the iPhone is a flagship mostly because of the kind of camera and photo quality it possesses. But having a flagship without knowing how to use it is as good as not having it at all which is why a good book like this was written to make that learning phase easy on you. Through many hours of the best of research, you can finally be able to get the best results out of your device and use your iPhone 12 Pro to the best of its potential.

The amount of research put into writing this Guide was so that lovers of photography who have switched or are looking to switch to iPhone 12 Pro can get started with using both the basic and advanced features of their phones as soon as possible and use it to start producing photographs of startling effects.

As a photography lover, I love every moment of it. The iPhone has proven to be a life-changing experience for me because whenever I go for an evening walk, a movie night, a casual hang out with friends, or an official tour, there are always moments of interest that I want to document through photos. In such moments, having a professional camera is very useful for me, however, having my iPhone 12 Pro provides a great alternative to the professional camera since they are not easy to carry around with us everywhere.

While writing this Guide, I came across many hidden and not frequently used undiscovered features that many ordinary users will probably not be aware of or only probably stumble into in the course of trying to navigate their way through the phone. Some of these features are those used only by professionals who may not even be aware that the iPhone 12 Pro can do many of the things they think can only be achieved with their DSLR camera.

This book is a result of many hours of going through the iPhone some of which have some high learning curves because of their level of difficulty. These hidden features that many people may not realize they have in their hands and many more things are the things this book aims to share with you to take you to the pinnacle of photography.

Whether you are a beginner or photography savvy, you will find amazing content in this Guide to boost your skills and explore new things.

Chapter 1

☙❧☙❧☙❧

Introducing the iPhone 12 Pro

Two main types of smartphones have dominated the phone market, iPhone, and Android. I will not be giving you a detailed comparison between both specs, details of both and the pros and cons of them can already be found on the internet, but I will only tell you about my personal experience.

For me, it would not have been possible to achieve my dream of smartphone photography without my iPhone. Without my iPhone, I simply would not have taken so many great photographs. So, for anyone who wants to take their smartphone photography to the next level, having an iPhone in their hands can make quite a lot of difference.

The most recent iPhones offered by Apple are as amazing as cell phones can be at this time. Apple has introduced four new phones in October 2020, namely: iPhone 12, iPhone 12 mini, iPhone 12 Pro, and iPhone 12 Pro max.

This means that there will be a lot more options for users to choose from. But in this book, we will be focusing our attention on the iPhone 12 Pro. It is in a phone that is in a class of its own because of its prominent refreshed design, amazing, powerful performance with the latest chip and processor, taking photography to the next level with the help of pro cameras, lightning-fast 5G, wireless charging, and sturdy screen (due to ceramic shield protection technology).

Apple has finally given us something that may not be so breathtaking, but rather gives a refreshing look. With the addition of widgets and freedom of default app choice, you feel more comfortable with it than ever before. Along with that, the privacy changes are a welcome development, and Apple has always been keen on providing its users a friendly touch. And the most amazing part of this iOS 14 update is that it is compatible with all the previously existing iPhone models along with all of these changes. So, this is excellent news for all the existing and new iPhone users as they can experience this new look together. In a nutshell, all of these changes are worth it, and it's time to say goodbye to the outdated, rigid grid.

iPhone 12 Pro will be love at first sight for the people who love photography or more specifically, smartphone photography because of its advanced camera features. It has a triple-lens camera (the third lens provides the zooming function). The thing that dramatically improves the photography experience in iPhone 12 Pro is the LiDAR sensor (Light Detection and Ranging Sensor). This sensor enables the camera to measure distances or ranges more efficiently, take pro-level photos in the dark, and provide faster performance.

All in all, the iPhone 12 Pro is an ideal choice for people interested in photography and don't want to buy a huge sized or very costly smartphone.

iPhone 12 Pro Display and Design at a Glance

iPhone 12 lineup introduction got the most prominent and dramatic design upgrade it has seen in many years. This design shows a clear distinction from the typical design Apple has shown these few past years.

The new iPhone 12 Pro has flat metal edges, which resemble the design of vintage models like the iPhone 5s or the models before that. It also has a glass front and back, but retained the textured matte finish of the iPhone 11 Pro.

These flat stainless-steel edges, gleaming like jewels, gives the phone a more distinguished and premium look.

iPhone12 Pro is covered by a layer of a ceramic shield, which is Apple's new technology for the protection of the phone to make it more rigid and according to the company, this shield makes the iPhone four times sturdier than its forerunners, meaning it has more chances of surviving a drop without getting any crack, breaking or scratches.

Apple further improved the iPhone 12 Pro's design by keeping the size smaller but providing a bigger and better

Super Retina XDR OLED 6.1-inch display; this was achieved by reducing the bezel (the borders that frame the screen) to make more room for the display. The front screen still has a top-notch where the front camera and face ID tech sensors are located. When changing from an older iPhone having an LCD, the display changes can be seen due to local dimming while watching a movie's dark scene.

Another notable thing is that the iPhone 12 Pro design is further supplemented by different colors, especially the pacific blue variant. The iPhone 12 Pro is also available in silver, gold, and graphite color.

What's New?

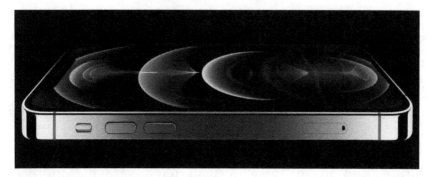

This is a very lucky year for the iPhone users, as the complete iPhone 12 line-up got some serious upgrades in design, features, and hardware.

The iPhone 12 Pro can be called the cream of this line-up with its out-of-world features, a stainless steel frame with shiny flat sides to give it a premium feel; a huge 6.1-inch Retina XDR display; a small notch and more screen with high pixel density, which enables you to have a cinema-like experience.

It also features a rocket-fast A14 bionic chip with a powerful processor that has never been seen ever before to run your games and other applications at full potential without any lags or glitches.

Also included is the latest 5G technology for fast downloads and browsing; a new camera system with amazing features to take the day and night photography to the next level; some newly added features like LiDAR sensor and ProRAW, increased RAM and huge storage space so that you can store anything you want in your phone; a strong body, which is protected by the Apple's new protection technology known as Ceramic Shield which makes it four times stronger than the former models.

With all these, Apple has taken a huge leap towards the future, and in my view, it will reign supreme in the upcoming time with all these super amazing features.

Basic Overview of Changes

The iPhone 12 Pro comes with a ton of major overhaul, especially in terms of its design. These newly introduced features are designed by Apple to make your user experience with the iPhone 12 Pro a great one.

There has been a nostalgic touch in the iPhone 12 Pro designs as it leans towards the earlier models, especially iPhone 5. The iPhone lovers still cannot forget that lovely design and feel given to the iPhone 5. Consequently, the iPhone 12 Pro design, although not the same, gives users a similar feel.

The notch has been reduced to make the screen larger, and the iOS has been upgraded.

Most improvements were made to the camera, it comes with three lenses with bigger apertures than before - 4x optical zoom, 10x digital zoom, and LiDAR sensors with improved AR technology, a seven-element lens for improved image processing and camera, and new features like ProRAW enabling you to add your required enhancements to the photos to satisfy your inner artist.

The latest internet technology, 5G, which the world is still thinking about, has been launched on the iPhone 12 Pro. According to Apple, it has a stronger screen and body than the previous versions. Their new Ceramic Shield technology gives it four times better protection from drops.

iPhone 12 Pro Tech Specs

Apple has brought a lot of new exciting features and hardware changes in its most recent line-up. If you are someone who is switching from Android to iPhone 12 Pro or an existing iPhone user and finding it hard to get used to these newly introduced changes in tech specs and design of iPhone 12 Pro, let me walk you through all the new changes - technical aspects and specifications.

Available Colors

iPhone 12 Pro is available in 4 colors

- Silver
- Graphite
- Gold
- Aqua Blue.

Storage

There are three variants as per storage space

- 128 GB
- 256 GB
- 512 GB

Physical Attributes

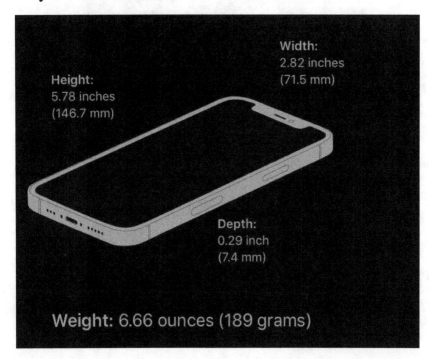

- Height 5.78 inches (146.7mm)
- Width 2.82 inches (71.5mm)
- Depth 0.29 inch (7.4mm)
- Weight 6.66 ounces (189 grams)

Screen

- Super Retina XDR Display
- 6.1 Inches

- 2532 x 1170 Resolution
- 440 pi Pixel Density
- High Definition Resolution Display
- True tone
- Wide Color
- Haptic Touch

Resistant to Water and Dust

With a rating of IP68, the iPhone 12 Pro can withstand any splash water and dust resistance rating is high, which means it can stay at 6-meter depth in water for up to 30 minutes.

RAM

The iPhone 12 Pro has 6 GB RAM.

Processor or Chip

The latest technology of Apple, the A14 Bionic chip, is installed on the iPhone 12 Pro.

Camera

It has three 12 Megapixels triple-lens camera system

- 12 MP Ultra-wide-angle lens has an f/2.4 aperture, five-element lens, and 120 FOV (field of vision)
- 12 MP Wide angle lens has an f/1.6 aperture and 7-element lens.
- 12 MP Telephoto lens has an f/2.0 aperture and a 6-element lens.

The iPhone 12 Pro has a 4x optical zoom in and zooms out the range, and with a digital zoom range of about 10x.

It contains a LiDAR scanner to provide the best experience in night mode.

The portrait mode helps you capture photos with a clear focus on the subject and blurred background with bokeh and depth-control.

It has a portrait lightening feature which comes with six different effects

- Natural
- Studio
- Contour
- Stage
- Stage- mono
- High key – mono

The wide and telephoto lens provides dual optical image stabilization.

It has a vibrant true tone with a slow sync flash.

Panorama shot (up to 63 megapixels).

A new wide-angle has 100% focus pixels.

Lens covers are made of sapphire crystals.

Night mode assists in low light by using wide and ultra-wide lenses.

It enables a deep fusion mode by using wide ultra-wide and telephoto lenses.

Smart HDR 3

Apple ProRAW*

This is a feature of ultra-wide lens correction.

Red-eye correction advance version.

Photo geotagging.

Auto image stabilization.

Burst mode

Photos are taken in two formats JPEG and HEIF

Video Recording Mode

HDR video can record up to 60 fps.

It supports 4k video, recording up to 24, 30, and 60 fps.

It can record HD 1080p video up to 30 and 60 fps.

It can record HD 720p video up to 30 fps.

A wide lens is used for the optical image stabilization for the video.

It has a 4x optical zoom range and a 6x digital zoom range.

Audio zoom filters out the unwanted noise from the surroundings.

Video mode also has a vibrant true tone flash.

Take pictures while recording a video without switching modes by using Quick Take video.

It supports slow-motion video for 1080p at 120 fps and 240 fps.

It also supports time-lapse shots in night mode.

To record better-looking videos in challenging surroundings. Extended dynamic range is used in iPhone 12 Pro.

Cinematic video stabilization at 4k, 1080p and 720p.

Autofocus throughout the video.

Up to 8 megapixels shots can be taken while recording 4k videos.

The feature of playback zoom.

The feature of stereo recording.

There are two video recording formats, HVEC and H.246.

True Depth Camera

The true depth camera is the latest face identification technology. It projects 30,000 invisible dots to create a detailed map of your face. It also takes an infrared photo of your face. All the specs and features mentioned in the camera section are also available in the true depth camera.

Networks

- 5G
- Wi-Fi 6

- Bluetooth 5.0

Ports

Single port for charger and hands-free.

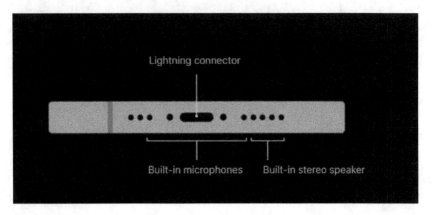

SIM Card

Dual Sim (Nano-Sim and e-Sim)

Note: The iPhone 12 Pro is not compatible with the existing SIM cards.

iPhone 12 Pro Operating System

The latest operating system used on the iPhone 12 Pro is iOS 14.1

iOS 14 Basic Overview

In the previous software updates, Apple focused on giving updates that provided more stability and speed, but they have come up with something that will shake its stabilized and established norms. It has brought a lot of changes that are going to change to the basic homely look, and the things you are used to seeing, but the best thing about this kind is that it is optional. And if something doesn't feel home to you, then you can simply opt-out of it, but there are plenty that you will love and are surely worth the try.

iOS 14 looks brand new. Feels like home. According to Apple's brand statement, iOS 14 is unique, with all-new features with a rediscovered look and design. They have made it user friendly more than ever before with the use of amazing new techniques and artificial intelligence that will enable the application you use frequently adjust themselves with ease to give you a personalized touch.

They have also added some cool new things like a picture in picture video mode, transition apps, intelligent new widgets, and freedom of choice to switch the default app for getting your daily tasks done like emailing, etc.

If we take a deep look at the changes and features introduced in this iOS 14 update, it seems to be one of Apple's most significant updates in recent times, and it has completely re-shaped the things your iPhone can do.

Home Screen and Widgets

The home screen of the iPhone has never changed since it was first introduced in 2007. There was that same Grid in which the icons were stacked in a row, and the only changeable option was the order, which looked boring and outdated because of the uniformity. But the good thing is that if we use all the new widgets and app library features iOS 14 has come up with, your home screen isn't going to look the same ever again.

App Library

You can access this newly introduced library feature that will automatically stash all your alphabetical order applications by swiping to the right. And in addition to that, it allows you to remove the extra apps from your home screen and add them to it.

You do not have to delete the less used apps to keep them away from your home screen. Simply long-press on the app icon and move it to the app library by clicking the newly added feature instead of deleting or hiding it. And that's not all: you can even hide or banish a complete page out of your home screen by simply long-pressing the home screen and clicking on the three dots that appear at the bottom, which will allow you to un-tick the pages you don't want.

Compact User Interface

Apple has given us a long-awaited but very much needed update in iOS 14 by introducing the compact user interface, which has rectified many issues Apple users were facing for the past many years. Few of the significant features of these changes are

- **Phone Calls**
- **Face Time Calls**
- **SIRI**
- **Picture in Picture**
- **Third-Party Apps**

Phone Calls

Now the calls will not take you away from your loved task by covering up the whole screen; instead, it will appear as a compact notification that will allow you to answer or reject it right from that with a simple swipe. Swiping up on it will dismiss the call, and if you choose to swipe down, it will take you to the whole standard screen where you can access all the standard features just like in the past.

Face Time Calls

The same is the case here, as mentioned above, for the phone calls. Suppose someone calls you on face time and you are going through an Instagram video or playing a game. In that case, it will appear at the top as a compact notification while you can continue your work, and then you can choose to either pick up that call or reject it by simply swiping up or down as per your choice. Swiping up will dismiss the call and swiping down will again take you to the face time main menu where you can perform any action within the app as you please.

SIRI

Apple has made SIRI more compact and up to date than ever before. It will not pop up on your home screen; instead, it will just give the piece of information you have asked for in the form of a small notification at the top corner of the screen where you can read it while performing your task very quickly.

Picture in Picture

Apple has introduced another cool feature that will allow you to take a call while watching a video or watching a video while going through the emails. It enables you to resize, move and minimize the split window appearing on your screen by simply pinching it or squeezing it with your fingers, and you can close it by swiping it off your screen. The finest part is you can continue to listen to audios and watch videos in your background.

Third-Party Applications

Third-Party applications like Skype have access to act as other iPhone calls and appear in the notification bar in a compact manner that is easy to manage.

Messages

Remaining linked with your loved ones is more critical than ever before. Apple pledges to take care of your every pain, and this time they have come up with a better way to help you stay in touch through their built-in messaging app.

With the amazing new features, you can stay updated on your group and individual conversations that matter the most. Moreover, it has given you multiple options to express yourself, whichever way you like. Be it in a group, mentions, or a simple inline reply.

A few of the fantastic features this app comes with are as follows:

- Group memoji icons
- Mentions
- Unique new stickers and emojis
- An option to pin favorite conversations

to the face time main menu where you can perform any
action within the app as you please.

SIRI

Apple has made SIRI more compact and up to date than
ever before. It will not pop up on your home screen;
instead, it will just give the piece of information you have
asked for in the form of a small notification at the top
corner of the screen where you can read it while
performing your task very quickly.

Picture in Picture

Apple has introduced another cool feature that will allow
you to take a call while watching a video or watching a
video while going through the emails. It enables you to
resize, move and minimize the split window appearing on

your screen by simply pinching it or squeezing it with your fingers, and you can close it by swiping it off your screen. The finest part is you can continue to listen to audios and watch videos in your background.

Third-Party Applications

Third-Party applications like Skype have access to act as other iPhone calls and appear in the notification bar in a compact manner that is easy to manage.

Messages

Remaining linked with your loved ones is more critical than ever before. Apple pledges to take care of your every pain, and this time they have come up with a better way to help you stay in touch through their built-in messaging app.

With the amazing new features, you can stay updated on your group and individual conversations that matter the most. Moreover, it has given you multiple options to express yourself, whichever way you like. Be it in a group, mentions, or a simple inline reply.

A few of the fantastic features this app comes with are as follows:

- Group memoji icons
- Mentions
- Unique new stickers and emojis
- An option to pin favorite conversations

MAPS

MAPS is one of the most amazing and cool features many smartphones have come up with to help us with navigation. Apple understands it's important, and they have revamped the inbuilt application to help you explore and navigate through the world amicably and amazingly. You can now quickly discover new parts of the world by customized settings to choose your traveling mode, be it cycling or electric cars, and get the best routes to your destination.

Translate

If you are a photographer or love traveling worldwide, Apple has introduced an amazing inbuilt application that will help you a great deal. With iPhone's Translate app, you can now get designed conversations in up to 11 different languages.

It has come up with different modes like hand mode, conversation mode, or attention mode to help you navigate different conversations simultaneously and come up with exact translations to understand the text.

Privacy

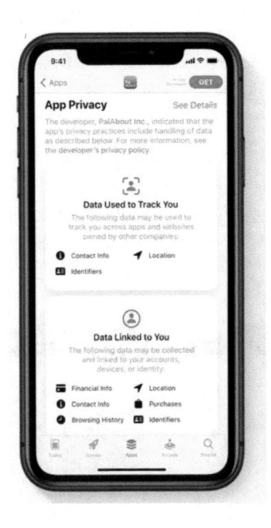

Few of those key features introduced by Apple to keep your privacy intact and transparent are as follows

- A Recording Indicator
- Approximate Location
- Transparent information on App Store
- Photo Library Controlled Access

Camera

Over the years, Apple has beefed up its camera a lot, taking its place in the market as one of its trademarks. If we look at the key improvements Apple, over the years, has done for the photography lovers in the camera lens, design, and application, we would say it is one of their hallmarks. And this time, in iOS 14, they have gone beyond the limits by proving impeccable changes and unique new features to make their camera stand out. Few of the newly introduced and revamped features are as follows:

- The beefed-up shot-in performance
- Video mode fast toggles
- Enhanced capturing experience in Night Mode

- Volume button enabled to take a quick video and burst shots
- Front camera enabled for mirrored photos

Apart from that, Apple has many notable changes in the other apps as well as upgrading and revamping of a few existing ones.

Pros

- Messaging becomes more comfortable& compatible with some other rivals
- A revamped home screen experience
- Freedom to choose their default app
- SIRI is smarter than ever before
- The Camera is faster and better

Cons

- The newly introduced app library is hard to manage and get used to
- A lot of new bugs, especially in widgets
- Several new complex & hidden features

Battery

Apple doesn't regularly expose the capacity of the battery, but we can infer that it has a capacity of 2815 mAh. Other battery specs include:

- Video playback up to 17 hours
- Video playback online up to 11 hours
- Audio Playback for up to 65 hours
- Wireless charging is also available

In the Box

As you unbox your new iPhone 12 Pro, you should expect to find the following items within:

- An iPhone with an iOS 14 operating system
- USB C-type lightning cable
- Manual of Operation

Chapter 2

ભજ૮ઝભજ૮ઝભજ

iPhone 11 Pro Camera with iPhone 12 pro

The latest iPhone 12 Pro has taken the place of the last model iPhone 11 Pro, which was released in the previous year. This newer version offers a new set of features and upgrades. In this section, we will compare both versions to see what new changes have been made and their effect on the performance of the new iPhone 12 Pro.

Design & Display

The most visible change between iPhone 12 Pro and iPhone 11 Pro is in their designs and screen sizes. Both phones have a small notch, reduced bezel display, and the same square-shaped rear camera system. But their designs are different, the iPhone 12 Pro has flat sides that look like jewels, while the iPhone 11 Pro has rounded sides. The flat sides provide a slimmer feel when compared to the rounded sides.

The iPhone 12 Pro has a screen of 6.1 inches, which is larger than the iPhone 11 Pro's 5.58 inches. There is also a difference in the resolution as iPhone 12 Pro has 460 PPI while the latter has 558 PPI. Besides, if we talk about the screen protection, then the iPhone 12 Pro is again the winner here as its screen has a layer of ceramic shield to save the screen from cracking when it falls.

Physical Properties

The height of the iPhone 12 Pro is 5.78 inches, which is a little more than the 5.67 inches of the iPhone 11 Pro. The former is 2.82 inches wide, and the latter has a width of 2.81 inches. There is a smaller difference of depth between the two models, the iPhone 12 Pro has a depth of 0.29 inches while iPhone 11 Pro has a depth of 0.32 inches. The iPhone 12 Pro with 189 grams is one gram heavier than the 188 grams iPhone 11 Pro.

Water and Dust Resistance

Both models are equipped with the latest and most proficient splash water and dust resistance rating, which is IP68 under IEC standard 60529. However, there is still a small difference between the two, that is, iPhone 12 Pro can stay in water up to a depth of 6 meters for 30 minutes, but the 11 Pro can only stay at 4 meters for 30 minutes.

Networks

The iPhone 12 Pro is a pioneer in this regard as it supports the 5G technology, which is the fastest technology in the present era and will be available to people in the future. This is one of the main features with which no other phone can be compared with the iPhone 12 series. The iPhone 11

Pro only supports a 4G LTE network; both phones support Wi-Fi 6 and Bluetooth 5.0.

Camera

iPhone 12 Pro Vs iPhone 11 Pro

There have been major improvements in this aspect in iPhone 12 Pro. There is a triple rear camera system in the iPhone 12 Pro, which has a 12 megapixels sensor, which is larger than the 12 MP sensor of the iPhone 11 Pro. The apertures of the ultra-wide lenses are wider, which allows the camera to reflect more light and increases the quality of the photos. In addition to that, Apple has introduced some new features in the iPhone 12 Pro, like the LiDAR sensor. This sensor has improved the camera function in the iPhone 12 Pro by a huge margin. The LiDAR sensor helps with low light situations in all modes available in the camera app, and it has also taken the AR technology to heights that have never been seen before. The phone can record videos at 4k 60 fps, but there is another difference, which is the "DOLBY VISION." The iPhone 12 Pro can record the same quality video with Dolby vision as well.

Processor

The chipset, which was used in iPhone 11 Pro was a 7nm A13 Bionic chipset; though it was unmatched during its time among all its peers, with the release of the iPhone 12 Pro, it is no longer the best. The iPhone 12 Pro has a 5nm A14 chipset, which, according to Apple, is the fastest and strongest GPU in this generation. The iPhone 11 Pro cannot be compared with iPhone 12 Pro in this regard as iPhone 12 Pro has an improved CPU, GPU, and image processor.

Storage

With the improvements and innovation in the technology, more storage space is required in the phones as the images, videos, and apps are getting larger. The iPhone 12 Pro has 128 GB storage in its base variant, which is two times more than the iPhone 11 Pro's base variant. However, the 512 GB variant is available in both versions.

Battery

The iPhone 12 Pro's battery life is 17 hours of playback time, which is less than 18 hours playback time given by iPhone 11 Pro, and both provide 65 hours of audio playback time. Therefore, the iPhone 12 Pro is better in this regard.

Unique Features of iPhone 12 Pro

iPhone 12 Pro has lots and lots of features similar to the iPhone 11 Pro, but there are some features which are unique to iPhone 12 Pro, such as:

- Fast 5G
- Fastest Processor
- Faster Auto-Focus
- Tougher Screen
- Faster Charging

It is the first phone that supports 5G, and 5G is a network for people who like everything very fast. This is the era of 5G as it will provide the fastest speeds when playing games, watching videos, or downloading anything.

The A14 Bionic chip provides the intense power that makes the iPhone 12 Pro have the kind of speed and capacity that enables it to load apps and games faster. It also helps run the improved camera and image processing capabilities of the phone more efficiently.

The iPhone 12 Pro is armed with a triple rear camera system, a front camera, and Smart HDR 3 intelligence function. Nevertheless, the main feature is the LiDAR sensor, which helps take photos in low light and provides a fast auto-focus function.

The ceramic shield makes the iPhone 12 Pro 4 times tougher.

The iPhone 12 Pro has a MagSafe accessory, which enables super-fast charging. MagSafe charges at two times the speed of normal charging pads, making the charging process easier.

Specifications	iPhone 12 Pro	iPhone 11 Pro
Colors	Pacific Blue, Gold, Graphite, Silver	Midnight Green, Silver, Space Gray, Gold
Storage	128GB, 256GB, 512GB	64GB, 256GB, 512GB
Display	Super Retina XDR Display	Super Retina XDR Display
	6.1-inch OLED screen (Diagonal)	5.8-inch OLED screen (Diagonal)
	2532 x 1170 resolution, 460ppi	2436 x 1125 resolution, 458ppi
	True Tone Display	True Tone Display
	800 nits max brightness typically	800 nits max brightness typically
	1200 nits max brightness in HDR	1200 nits max brightness in HDR
Physical Attributes: Dimensions (Height, Width, Depth, and Weight)	5.78 inches (146.7 mm)	5.67inches (144.0 mm)
	2.82 inches (71.5mm)	2.81 inches (71.4 mm)
	0.29 inch (7.4 mm)	0.32 inch (8.1 mm)
	6.66 ounces (189 grams)	6.63 ounces (188 grams)
Water and Dust Resistant	Rated IP68 (maximum depth of 6 meters up to 30 minutes) under IEC standard 60529	Rated IP68 (maximum depth of 4 meters up to 30 minutes) under IEC standard 60529
Chip	A14 Bionic chip	A14 Bionic chip
	Next-generation Natural Engine	Next-generation Natural Engine

Specifications	iPhone 12 Pro	iPhone 11 Pro
Camera	Pro 12 MP camera system (Ultra-Wide and Telephoto)	Triple 12 MP camera system (Ultra-Wide and Telephoto)
	Ultra-Wide: f/2.4 aperture	Ultra-Wide: f/2.4 aperture
	Wide: f/1.6 aperture	Wide: f/1.8 aperture
	Telephoto: f/2.0 aperture	Telephoto: f/2.0 aperture
	Night Mode	Night Mode
	Deep Fusion	Deep Fusion
	Apple ProRAW	None
	Dual optical image stabilization	Dual optical image stabilization
	2x optical zoom in, 2x optical zoom out; 4x optical zoom range Digital zoom up to 10x	2x optical zoom in, 2x optical zoom out; 4x optical zoom range Digital zoom up to 10x
	Bright True Tone flash with Slow Sync	Bright True Tone flash with Slow Sync
	Night Mode portraits	None
	Portrait Lighting with six effects	Portrait Lighting with six effects
	(Natural, Studio, Contour, Stage, Stage Mono, High- Key Mono)	(Natural, Studio, Contour, Stage, Stage Mono, High- Key Mono)
	Smart HDR 3 for photos	Next-generation Smart HDR for photos

Specifications	iPhone 12 Pro	iPhone 11 Pro
Video Recording	4K video recording at 24 fps, 30 fps, or 60 fps	4K video recording at 24 fps, 30 fps, or 60 fps
	1080p HD video recording at 30 fps or 60 fps	1080p HD video recording at 30 fps or 60 fps
	HDR video recording with Dolby Vision up to 60 fps	____
	Extended dynamic range for video up to 60 fps	Extended dynamic range for video up to 60 fps
	Optical image stabilization for video	Optical image stabilization for video
	2x optical zoom in, 2x optical zoom out	2x optical zoom in, 2x optical zoom out
	Digital zoom up to 6x	Digital zoom up to 6x
	Audio zoom	Audio zoom
	QuickTake video	QuickTake video
	Night mode Time-lapse	____
	Slo-mo video support for 1080p at 120 fps or 240 fps	Slo-mo video support for 1080p at 120 fps or 240 fps
	Time-lapse video with stabilization	Time-lapse video with stabilization
	Stereo recording	Stereo recording
Front Camera	True Depth camera	True Depth camera
	12 MP photos	12 MP photos
	f/2.2 aperture	f/2.2 aperture

Specifications	iPhone 12 Pro	iPhone 11 Pro
	Retina Flash	Retina Flash
	Smart HDR 3 for photos	Next-generation Smart HDR for photos
	Portrait mode with advanced bokeh and Depth Control	Portrait mode with advanced bokeh and Depth Control
	Portrait Lighting with six effects (Natural, Studio, Contour, Stage, Stage Mono, High-Key Mono)	Portrait Lighting with six effects (Natural, Studio, Contour, Stage, Stage Mono, High-Key Mono)
	Extended dynamic range for video at 30 fps	Extended dynamic range for video at 30 fps
	Cinematic video stabilization (4K, 1080p, and 720p)	Cinematic video stabilization (4K, 1080p, and 720p)
	4K video recording at 24 fps, 30 fps, or 60 fps	4K video recording at 24 fps, 30 fps, or 60 fps
	HDR video recording with Dolby Vision up to 30 fps	____
	1080p HD video recording at 30 fps or 60 fps	1080p HD video recording at 30 fps or 60 fps
	Slo-mo video support for 1080p at 120 fps	Slo-mo video support for 1080p at 120 fps
	Night mode	____
	Deep Fusion	____

Specifications	iPhone 12 Pro	iPhone 11 Pro
	QuickTake video	QuickTake video
	Animoji and Memoji	Animoji and Memoji
Cellular and Wireless	GSM/EDGE	GSM/EDGE
	UMTS/HSPA+	UMTS/HSPA+
	DC-HSDPA	DC-HSDPA
	CDMA EC-DO Rev. A (some models)	CDMA EC-DO Rev. A (some models)
	5G (sub-6 GHz and mm-Wave)	___
	Gigabit LTE	Gigabit LTE
	Wi-Fi 6 (802.11ax) with MIMO	Wi-Fi 6 (802.11ax) with MIMO
	Bluetooth 5.0	Bluetooth 5.0
	Ultra-Wideband chip for spatial awareness	Ultra-Wideband chip for spatial awareness
	Built-in GPS, GLONASS, Galileo, QZSS, and BeiDou	Built-in GPS/GNSS
	VoLTE	VoLTE
	NFC with reader mode	NFC with reader mode
	Express Cards with the power reserve	Express Cards with the power reserve
	Wi-Fi calling	Wi-Fi calling
Power and Battery	Built-in rechargeable lithium-ion battery	Built-in rechargeable lithium-ion battery
	MagSafe and Qi wireless charging	Qi wireless charging

Specifications	iPhone 12 Pro	iPhone 11 Pro
	Charging via USB to a computer system or power adapter	Charging via USB to a computer system or power adapter
	Video playback up to 17 hours	Video playback up to 18 hours
	Video playback (streaming) up to 11 hours	Video playback (streaming) up to 11 hours
	Audio Playback up to 65 hours	Audio Playback up to 65 hours
	Fast- charge capable	Fast- charge capable
Sensors	LiDAR Scanner	___
	Three-axis gyro	Three-axis gyro
	Accelerometer	Accelerometer
	Proximity sensor	Proximity sensor
	Ambient light sensor	Ambient light sensor
	Barometer	Barometer

Chapter 3

CʒꙄCʒꙄCʒꙄ

Smartphone Photography Overview

"Knowledge of Photography is just as important as that of the alphabet. The illiterate of the future will be ignorant of the use of camera and pen alike."

Laszlo Moholy–Nagy 1923

Introduction to Photography

What is photography? This question seems simple, but it's not. It is like asking what the meaning of life is. Everyone has a different answer to this question; for some people, photography is an art; for others, it is a profession or a hobby, and for some people, it is like meditation. That's because Photography is very complex that encompasses many aspects. It encompasses focus, imagination, and creativity, and it differs from person to person.

But in layman's terms, photography can be defined as the art of capturing light with a camera's help to form an image. To imagine the world without photos is very hard.

Photographs have become an integral part of this world. Photography helps us in preserving history, our best family moments like the first steps our child took, scenery, or species of animals or plants that will become extinct soon. Mothers, especially, put a lot of effort into creating complete albums just to protect their precious memories.

Photographs call up the essence of the places we once visited or the places, we have never been to, or the places, we will never visit. So, photographs truly make up a lot of our world.

By taking a closer look at the essence of photography, even the people who are not familiar with it can appreciate and relate to pictures. But if you want to take professional photos, you will need lots of expensive gear such as:

- Camera
- Lenses
- Editing and processing software
- Other accessories, including tripods, filters, and flash.

All of this will require a lot of money, and you will have to take care of them and carry this gear all the time with you.

It will not be feasible for everyone, especially the people who are not professional photographers. But do not worry, for every problem, there is always a solution, and this problem can be solved easily with your smartphone.

Smartphone Photography

In this day and age, most of us keep a mobile phone with us all the time, which means we always have a camera with us. We just need to master it perfectly to open a whole new world of possibilities and opportunities.

With the improvements being made every day in the designs and specs, the smartphone can do a good job. To capture a great photo, you need a good device, and you have to be in the right place at the right time.

In short, you need a perfect opportunity, and with a good smartphone, you can easily avail all these opportunities. Even if you are traveling, or you are somewhere on vacation, on a bike trip, just taking a walk, going out with friends or family, or going from office to work or school, your smartphone is always with you, and you can capture all the special moments you want to preserve.

The next question will be which phone to use to get the maximum out of smartphone photography? Let me give you a short overview. The qualities you should be looking for in a smartphone are its design, processor, storage, and the things necessary for photography like image quality, resolution, megapixels battery, image stabilization, etc.

We all know that smartphone cameras are not even close to professional cameras. They are not efficient or strong like a DSLR, the pixels are low, and there are not many manual controls or tools for fine-tuning and even lack many editing applications like Adobe Photoshop. So, where is the advantage in that? Do not think that you cannot achieve great Photography by just using a phone; you can search your way through the internet.

You will find that a lot of people are already doing it. Despite the absence of complex manual controls and editing apps, you can work more on innovation and composition. Just go back to the basics, think more about the light and colors, give some thought to the lines and the placement of the subject, and it will work wonders for you.

I see people taking photos with their phones every day, and I know most of them are always disappointed with the photos they take, but it does not happen because of the device or the camera. It happens because they do not approach it the right way. An intelligent artist who knows precisely how to utilize everything in his view in the best possible way can create wonderful photos with just a smartphone camera.

Develop Professional Photography Skills

These are some of the skills which can help you improve your photography skills immediately. Just keep practicing these skills to become a professional photographer.

Following others can be a very effective starting skill for new photographers. Observing other professional artists' work and immersing yourself in their work can help you learn a lot about photos. You can get some ideas about what to shoot, the composition, and when you should take a photograph.

The best place to keep an eye on these artists will be social media sites, especially Instagram; there are many talented artists on this website, so you can choose the artists you like.

To keep things simple, just focus on taking simple and captivating photos; such photos depend on your subject and composition. The choice of placement or arrangement of the subject in the image is called composition. The rule of the third can be used for the better composition of the photo. Try not to put the subject in the center of the image; setting it on the side has proven to be more interesting.

Whenever we are taking a photo, our natural inclination is to place the subject in the middle of the frame, and this is one of the biggest mistakes that beginners make.

Turn on the Grid mode on your smartphone; it will break the image into three parts in three rows and columns and create nine equal sections; to get a better picture, try placing the subject along the lines of intersection points. This rule can be applied to capture the picture of a landscape and even a person.

Train your eyes to become a good photographer; imagining the picture even before taking it helps you create better photos and look for opportunities in the environment like leading lines, natural frames, reflections, and symmetry. All of these visual factors will add depth to your Photography and help you create interesting photos.

Leading lines can effectively attract viewers' attention towards your subject; leading lines can be found everywhere around you, such as the lines drawn on a road and guard rails of the stairs.

Symmetry can mesmerize a person. It ranges from architecture, natural settings like mountains, rows of trees, or deserts.

Reflections can be used innovatively to see your subject from a new angle. A reflection of a beautiful hill in a still lake can help you create an amazing image.

Framing can be used to direct the focus of viewers wherever you want them to focus. Doors, trees, arches, windows, opening between two stones, and many other shapes can be used as frames to add more story to your images.

There are specific times of the day when you can find an opportunity to create something intriguing, especially at sunrise and sunset. This is also known as the golden hour by professional photographers; many of them wait to take some gorgeous pictures at this time of the day.

Sometimes getting closer to the subject can give you surprisingly good pictures. Start from a wide range and keep getting closer to the subject and take multiple photos; you will be able to discern a lot of details from these images.

Changing the angle while taking a photo might give you a pleasant surprise. We see the world from our eye level, so taking a picture from a higher or lower angle will be a very interesting experience.

Use natural light effectively and keep the flash mostly off to create a more natural environment in the picture. Flash is best used when the sun is right at the top of your head, and you need the flash to fill the shadows.

Use a good editing app to give a finishing touch to your photos.

Camera Apps to Use

There are bundles of apps on an iPhone that can be used for photography, but we will only require three types of them.

- Camera Apps (to click photos).
- Editing Apps
- Pictures Sharing Apps

Even though the built-in camera app on the iPhone is amazing, sometimes you require a little more control, such as some manual tuning like controlling the shutter speed or ISO, etc.

Some popular iPhone third party apps for the camera, editing, and sharing of cool photos are as follows:

- Snap seed (photo editing app with a huge arsenal of tools)
- VSCO (An app to add filters)
- Touch Retouch (Editing app mainly to remove unwanted objects from the picture)
- After light 2 (Editing app for people who want to move beyond the basic level)
- Adobe Lightroom CC (An editing app for the professionals)
- Camera +2 (best camera app with manual controls)
- Mextures (an app to add texture to the photos)

Apple Photography Revamped

Apple has introduced a lot of changes to the iPhone with the iOS 14.1 update. In this update, major improvements have been brought to the iPhone camera and photography, and Apple has pushed photography to the next level with all the new features and tools.

The three lenses (wide, ultra-wide, and telephoto lens) with optical and digital zoom and LiDAR sensors provide the best photography experience. Incredible night mode photos, sharp focus on the subject with blurred background, portrait lighting mode with six effects, dual optical image stabilization, enhanced red-eye correction, better true tone with slow sync flash, burst mode, with many other things to explore will take you on a journey which you have never experienced before.

Chapter 4

ଓଓଓଓଓଓ

iPhone 12 Pro Camera Overview

The iPhone 12 Pro is simply a device from the future, everything is undeniably brilliant, from its specifications to its design. There have been many iPhone 12 Pro updates, but the major improvements have occurred in the camera.

Using the iPhone 12 Pro camera will present a badass experience to people, especially those who love photography and video making. Saying that iPhone 12 pro is a time traveler from the future is not wrong because of the features it's offering such as LiDAR sensor, Dolby Vision, and 5G; all of these belong to the future, and trust me, all of these will become the most pursued features in the upcoming time while selecting a device.

iPhone 12 Pro camera has been equipped with a rich arsenal of futuristic characteristics that includes three heaven-defying lenses (wide, ultra-wide, telephoto), the LiDAR sensor to perceive and form a depth map of face and surroundings, a huge list of different modes for photography and video recording, very sharp autofocus, Dolby Vision HDR for vibrant videos, image stabilization, and many more of such surprises are waiting for everyone.

iPhone 12 Pro Camera's in Focus

The iPhone 12 Pro has three rear 12 Megapixels cameras. One of these three contains a wide-angle lens with an f/1.6 aperture, which can be used for dual detection of pixels and phase. The second one has a telephoto lens having an f/2.0 aperture and at last an ultra-wide lens with f/2.4 and 120 degrees field of vision. These cameras provide iPhone 12 Pro with 4x optical for zoom in and zoom out range and 10x digital for zoom in and zoom out range.

The selfie camera is located at the top-notch with the Face ID sensor. The 12 Megapixel selfie camera has an f/2.2 aperture and makes it possible to click some amazing selfies that can also be used for blogging and face identification.

One of the main selling points of the iPhone is the LiDAR sensor; the major function of the LiDAR sensor is to emit lasers and measure the distance between the subject and camera to provide better AR abilities and improved performance in low light. Accordingly, the Apple LiDAR sensor helps the camera to autofocus six times faster in the night mode.

With the help of so many features in the camera section, iPhone 12 Pro will be the first-ever smartphone in the world to allow you to record High Definition 4k videos at 60 frames per second by using Dolby Vision, which is a professional grade format and is used all over the world to make cinematic videos full of vibrant colors and life-like black and bright highlights.

Moreover, the Dolby Vision videos or trailers can be readily edited on the device itself, which has never been possible before in the history of smartphones; this must be great news for the people interested in the filmography.

Another killer feature for photography announced by Apple is ProRAW; it will be released later this year. You all must be wondering that "What is ProRAW?" As the name suggests, raw means something which has not been processed and is in its unprocessed or early form. Normally when we capture a photo from a DSLR or smartphone, computational photography is automatically applied to that photo. For those who do not know, computational photography means the ability of the camera to apply certain effects to the photo to make it appear enhanced beyond the information captured by the lenses and sensors.

There was a function introduced some time ago named RAW, which enabled us to take photos without those effects, and to get those effects, we need to shoot in JPEG format, but by shooting in JPEG format, we lose the chance of in-depth editing to get our required results. By shooting in RAW or JPEG, we will have to compromise on some things, but by introducing ProRAW, Apple wants to remove these limitations.

So, the ProRAW will capture RAW photos with some processing applied to them, through deep fusion, Smart HDR, and by the noise reduction effects. However, leaving the margin for further editing so we can make changes or enhance the photo exactly to our liking.

iPhone 12 Pro Camera Modes Overview

The iPhone 12 Pro enables you to take photos with such details and control that sometimes even you will be confused by the quality of those photos as they will surpass your expectations by a huge margin, along with the powerful triple camera, the iPhone 12 Pro has a lot of different modes to let your imagination run wild and discover the art of photography to the extreme.

The different modes available in the iPhone 12 Pro's Camera are as follows

- Night Mode
- Portrait Mode
- Burst Mode
- Selfie Mode
- Dolby Vision
- ProRAW Mode
- Quick Take Mode
- Smart HDR 3 Mode and Deep Fusion

The people who like to travel or simply go out with friends to enjoy the nightlife, such people are often faced with the trouble of low light when taking a picture, but there is no need to worry as the iPhone 12 Pro is a perfect choice for you because of its improved night mode feature.

The night mode has been enabled on all the lenses in iPhone 12 Pro, whether it's the wide, ultra-wide, telephoto, or selfie camera. The night mode automatically activates whenever you take a photo in low light conditions, but it can also be enabled manually by entering the settings.

The shutter speed will be set at default, but it can also be changed manually to some extent. So, iPhone 12 Pro provides you with a lot of control during night photography.

The major improvement in the night mode has been the LiDAR sensor's addition. LiDAR is a technology from the future, and NASA has been developing this technology to be used during their project on MARS. This is the key factor that allows the iPhone 12 Pro camera to work effectively even during low light conditions; the LiDAR sensor allows the autofocus to work at 6x speed during night mode.

Taking a selfie at night time or in the low light condition is also not a problem with iPhone 12 Pro, just open the front camera and make sure the phone is stable, and this will be enough for you to capture amazing selfies at any time.

Also, there is another good news for the people who like night time photography and who want to record a time-lapse shot during the night. Yes, with iPhone 12-night mode, capturing a time-lapse shot with a longer interval during night time is now possible!

The portrait mode was introduced with the iPhone 7 plus, it was hardly able to capture any decent quality picture. In short, there were a lot of issues with it, especially the edge detection issues; this mode improved with different updates even up to iPhone 11. With the iPhone 11 series, it became much better, even then it did not seem to still be good enough for savvy photography enthusiasts.

Sometimes, it will capture amazing photos, but other times, it will fail badly, and all of this happened due to the inability of the camera to precisely detect the edges and to differentiate the subject from the environment in a complex background.

The only solution to this problem was to add a sensor that can measure the depth in a space and create a map of it, and this is what Apple has exactly achieved in iPhone 12 Pro with the help of LiDAR sensor. Portrait mode is used to blur the background and focus on the subject; just touch the point on the screen you want the Camera to focus on.

With all the improvements, portrait mode can now also be used at night.

Taking action shots is never easy. I, too, struggle when taking action photos because it is very difficult to capture good photos of moving subjects, but the iPhone 12 Pro can make it very simple for you with the trick called the burst shot. The optimized burst shot with the help of a triple camera and automatic image stabilization lets you take multiple good photos in a row. This will help you to never miss a shot again in the future.

The art of smartphone photography cannot be called complete without counting the selfies; most people love to capture selfies no matter where they are and what they are doing. The selfie mode in iPhone 12 pro has been optimized with the help of a depth sensor, and it helps in taking very detailed and vibrant selfies. Night mode also allows you to capture selfies during low light conditions, which is a great boom for selfie lovers.

One of the most exciting features of the iPhone 12 Pro is its ability to record videos in Dolby Vision (High Dynamic Range), which means a greater range of colors are available than the standard range. The cinematic trailers are often recorded in Dolby Vision, so you can already imagine how the quality of the videos recorded in the format of Dolby vision will be so full of colors and life, and iPhone twelve has the honor of becoming the first smartphone to be able to directly record and edit the Dolby vision videos in the phone.

ProRAW mode is used to capture raw photos with some effects; these photos can be further edited by using Photoshop or other software.

There are sometimes when you are taking a photo, and something unexpected happens, and you want to record that particular thing, but switching between different modes will waste time, and you might miss the chance to record the event. With iPhone 12 Pro, you can easily record a video while capturing photos. T do that; you have to simply press the shutter button and not release it. Doing this will start the video recording without switching between photo and video mode, and this is known as a Quick Take video or Quick Take mode.

Another part of the iPhone 12 Pro camera's success is smart HDR 3 and deep fusion technology. This technology is available on all four cameras on the iPhone 12 pro. (Three at the rear and one at the front)

The smart HDR 3 and deep fusion technology provide maximum details, texture addition, and noise reduction to even separate parts of the photo with advanced machine learning and pixel by pixel processing of the photos. The main function of these technologies is to work out different details in different light conditions and then combine them to provide a better image; the deep fusion works in the dark while the smart HDR 3 comes into use in relatively sunnier conditions.

Switch between Different Lenses

The wide-angle lens has an f/1.6 aperture, and as its name suggests, wide-angle covers a large field of view. This wide range of view will allow the camera to capture the scene you are looking for in your camera. The wide-angle camera is best to use when taking a photo of some landscape, group or family photos, and street photography. It can also be used for action shots along with burst shots.

Ultra-Wide Lens

When a scene you are trying to capture with your camera cannot be adequately covered by the wide-angle, the iPhone 12 Pro allows you to use the semitransparent areas on the outer side of the frame to capture those sections.

If you see that there are objects outside the frame that you want in your photo, then switch to the Ultra-Wide-Angle lens f/2.4 aperture and 120-degree field of vision. In this mode, the objects outside of the transparent frame will be now be captured by the camera.

Wide lens

With the help of f/2.0 aperture, the telephoto lens provides 2x optical zoom in without any distortion, thus allowing you to capture objects that are far away without physically going near them. 10x digital zoom can also be used, but using it will reduce the quality of the photo.

iPhone 12 Pro Telephoto lens

The telephoto lens allows you to take more distinct shots of children or animals who are less likely to notice you because of the distance, and this way, the photo does not seem forced.

Chapter 5
ᏟᏋᏋ)ᏟᏋᏋ)ᏟᏋᏋ)

Basics of Capturing a Photo

Capturing a photo seems simple, for a lot of people, they think it is just to open the camera, point towards the subject in the frame, click the shutter button, and a photo is born. However, it's not so simple. Remember, there is a difference between a simple photo and a good photo. There are a lot of best practices you can follow to get good photos.

When capturing photos, the subject's position can make a lot of difference, if the subject is not properly placed, a good photo can turn into a bad one. Although the learning process can take some time for beginners, the iPhone 12 Pro provides the option of gridlines which, when enabled makes it easier for beginners to take quality pictures.

After enabling the grid lines, the next step will be to adjust the camera's focus on the subject, and normally, people think that covering only the subject in the frame will make the photo better. Still, from a professional point of view, the subject should only cover one-third of the frame; the rest two-third should be covered by negative space. This will make the subject stand out more in the background;

just make sure before pressing the shutter button on the screen; it is where you want the camera to focus.

Try different angles when taking pictures. It will allow you to see things differently, and it might add more depth and height to the photo and make it stick out more in the background.

Use everything in the environment to help you take great pictures, the symmetries, reflections, architectures, landscapes.

Use flash scarcely as it is most uncomfortable for the subject and hinders capturing the natural emotions and reactions. Moreover, when the light comes from the same place as the lens, it will remove the scene's natural shadow.

The telephoto lens provides you optical zoom and allows you to capture photos from a distance, but it is better not to use it. Instead, go closer to the subject manually, and this will allow you to see details that cannot be seen otherwise.

One of the most vital things to get good photos is the white balance. Sometimes you take a photo indoors, and it turns out that the skin color looks absurd. Mastering WB will help you solve this problem.

Using all these practices, you can convert a photo into a good one with the help of the iPhone 12 Pro camera.

Use of Different Modes

The iPhone 12 Pro is the first-ever smartphone to feature the 4K video quality with 60 frames per second high definition recording, Dolby vision, black and white highlights, and true colors. With all of that, it has multiple amazing modes that can help you take your photography endeavor to new heights. Some of those amazing modes that can help you in taking wonderful photos are as follows:

- Portrait Mode
- Night Mode
- ProRAW Mode
- Burst Mode
- Selfie Mode

Portrait Mode

Apple has taken Photography to the very next level, especially portrait and night mode photos, with the introduction of laser and LiDAR sensors in the iPhone 12 Pro.

Apple specially designed these sensors to support portrait mode and night mode photography. These sensors are built to help capture the iPhone 12 Pro camera perfect pictures in low and dim light areas by automatically enabling these sensors.

You can take the perfect portrait mode photo by following these steps:

Open your camera app; then you swipe right.

Next, you choose the portrait mode to select the subject you want to be in focus so that the camera could use the depth-in-field effect to help you take a photo with a sharp focus on the subject you selected and blur the rest of the background.

Lastly, wait for the on-screen light to turn yellow. Once it does, press the shutter button, and your perfect portrait mode photo is captured.

Night Mode

Apple has come up with a very unique and advanced night mode feature, which is an automatic and out-of-the-box idea, unlike most of the other smartphones as it gets triggered automatically, and you don't need to worry about figuring if there is a need for the night mode or not. iPhone 12 Pro's laser sensors will automatically detect the light around and automatically trigger the night mode if there is a need for it.

iPhone 12 Pro night mode vs iPhone 11 Pro without night mode

With the improved laser sensors in the iPhone 12 Pro camera, night mode works pretty fine and better than most of the competitors around to give you a stand-out result.

To take a phone in Night mode, all you have to do is get your camera open. It will automatically enhance the light around by enabling this feature to give you better overall exposure. Your photo becomes charming, full-of-colors, and has a visually great background along with your face.

ProRAW Mode

In the most recent updates of iOS, Apple has released some of the most promising and amazing camera features included in iPhone 12 Pro and Pro Max exclusively. With ProRAW mode, photography nerds and smartphones are going to be like a match made in heaven. So, if you are a photography lover and going to purchase or have purchased an iPhone 12 Pro, this is a feature that sets it apart from its other family members.

For iPhone photographers, this is one of the most promising releases ever. To use this feature, you will need to turn it on first, from the settings menu as Apple has added a new special toggle under the camera app section in settings for ProRAW mode with a warning that each of the photo files will be about 25MB or more so that only the pros should enable and use it.

Once you enable that feature going past the warning, there a piece of happy news waiting right within the camera app for you in the right corner as a RAW toggle; you can simply press that to enable this feature.

The RAW mode will help you take the editing of photos to the next level once you have taken them as it gives you the freedom to change color, add details, strong effects, white balance, and dynamic range into it. Apple aims to give you an extra touch of deep fusion and Smart High Definition Frame rate, along with all the other traditional features to take your photography experience to the next level.

Burst Mode

As we all know, Apple has brought a lot of new changes in its latest cell phone, iPhone 12 Pro's camera, and given photographers a new thing to explore. Its amazing features and additional sensors have already made their mark.

One of these cool features is the burst mode, which can be used to capture a perfect photo during an action. Photographers widely use this feature to click a perfect picture while doing a shoot or performing an action as it gives multiple angles without much of a hassle. So, explained here is how you can take a Burst mode picture without much of a hassle, and if you are an iPhone 12 Pro photography lover, you are going to love this feature.

This is all because, in the past, the introduction of the Quick Take video feature created a lot of problems for photographers who loved burst mode as the volume button was held to shoot. Thus, shutter button functions were given to the new Quick Take Video mode instead of Burst mode. Now, Apple has again fixed the issue and brought back the volume button feature, which is held to shoot as shutter button adjustments. So here is how you can take a burst mode photo now:

The first thing you need to do is tap the camera app on your iPhone 12 to open it and head towards settings.

Next, you go to the list and select the camera menu.

Next, enable the toggle in front of the feature and use the volume up for Burst.

Once you are done with the settings, head to the camera app and enjoy the burst mode by simply holding the volume up button. And now you don't have to worry anymore about accidentally enabling the quick take video mode or the hassle of tapping and dragging the shutter button; it's simpler and easier just like the way you will like.

Telephoto Lens

Apple first introduced this special lens in its iPhone 11 Pro variant and continued it in the newly released iPhone 12 Pro but with many new notable enhancements that will improve and take your photography passion to new heights.

This iPhone variant also has the exact f/2.0, 52mm Telephoto lens as the previous version, but Apple has added some cool new features to it, too, to make it even better. They are:

- Deep Fusion Effect
- LiDAR Sensor
- HDR Video at 60 frames per second

All of these cool features will allow you to take a great photo that will have an improved deep coloring effect, which will be fused better than ever before, and the additional LiDAR sensor will allow you to capture equally good photos in low light areas along with 6 times faster face detection to let you click a photo in an instant. And the 52mm Telephoto lens will allow you to zoom up to 10 times digitally and 2 times optically.

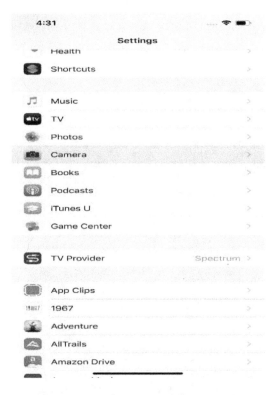

Advance Volume Buttons Uses

Apple has given its fans and especially iPhone photography lovers a great feature to use the volume up and down button as a shutter to capture a photo or record videos in a quick gesture.

It is a speed-boosting tip, which is widely used by smartphone photographers to take a quick and clean selfie or record a quick video with their iPhones' help. You can use this amazing feature by simply opening your camera app and clicking either of the buttons to take a photo.

And to add a flare to it, you can long-hold either of these buttons to start recording a video, and it will keep on recording as long as your button is pressed.

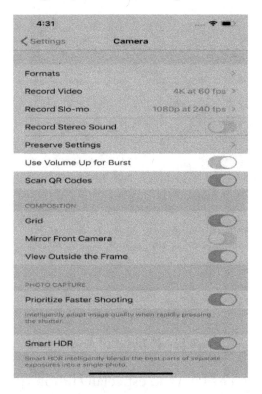

What's more, Apple has now made it possible for you to extend this further, especially if you are someone who wants to continue capturing your photo while in the middle of something else by using the burst mode feature the iPhone 12 Pro offers. This you can turn it on within the settings, and now, every time you will hold the volume down button, burst mode will start capturing the photos.

To do that, you simply head into the settings app on the iPhone 12 Pro menu, tap to open the camera app, and scroll down to where you will find "Use Volume for Burst" to turn on that feature by toggling the button on. You know it is on when the button is green.

Quick Take Mode

It is a recently introduced feature introduced by Apple that will let you take a quick photo, record a short video, or take several photos with the help of burst mode.

All of this can be done by either clicking or holding the volume button. You may open the camera app and hold down the white shutter button inside the camera to start recording a Quick Take video without enabling anything else.

Apple has given you complete control of whatever you want to do. With a single click of your shutter button will act as a button to take a photo or record a video as long as what you want is simply clicking it. It will let you know of the recording by turning from white to red. And the moment you will remove your finger, the recording stops.

Ultra-Wide Lenses for Ultra-Wide Photos.

If you are a photography enthusiast, love the iPhone and its camera and is willing to pay a few extra bucks for your photos to be amazing, Apple will not leave you disappointed as they have set the wide and ultra-wide lens just for you to get ultra pro photos in their iPhone 12 Pro camera.

Wide camera angle photos are the ones I personally love, and shooting them with the help of the iPhone 12 pro cameras gives an amazing up close and personal joy as they give you a wider field of view along with the object of focus being the center of attention. Photography lovers around the world enjoyed iPhone 11 Pro ultra-wide lens effects last year, and I as well enjoyed every single photo of it, be it a small indoor click or a widespread landscape snap.

Ultra-Wide lenses are known for giving you super fantastic landscape photos. Apple has introduced many new features in iPhone 12 Pro to aid the ultra-wide lenses, which will give you an amazing experience with complete sharpness and far less distortion than photographers suffered from the iPhone 11 Pro ultra-wide lens.

This time Apple has done their best in taking care of the problems photographers around the world faced while using the ultra-wide lens. The photos were taken in Phone 11 Pro usually gets blurred at the edges because of the ultra-wide angles. This time, with the iPhone 12 Pro, Apple has come up with a masterstroke by bringing in some software changes, that allows you to take clear and crisp photos with an edge to edge detail.

Zoom in and Zoom out Features

The iPhone 12 Pro camera comes up with 3 cameras with ultra-wide, wide, and telephoto lenses, which enables you to get way more customization and zoom than you can even imagine.

You can choose to zoom in and out by simply tapping on the 1x icon within the camera app. From here, you can see the different indicators with different zoom levels, which will allow you to choose between them from 1x to 5x and from 5x to even 10x digital zoom with the help of an ultra-wide lens.

Once you have chosen between the camera zooms and have successfully adjusted them to suit your need, simply swipe down on the wheel (that was helping you choose) to close or hide it and use the app normally by tapping or toggling as you deem convenient.

Chapter 6
෴෴෴

A Detailed View of Camera Settings

The iPhone 12 Pro offers a new design, camera, and some new internal features which will help you to capture amazing photos, even if the difference in the numbers between the cameras of the iPhone 12 Pro and previous versions does not seem much. There are deep fusion, LiDAR technology, smart HDR, and a lot of more interesting features.

Worthy of note is the fact that wide and ultra-wide aperture are f/1.6 and f/2.4 respectively this year, but this is quite a noteworthy increase as it will allow a lot more light to enter the lens.

In this section, I will guide you through some basic and advanced settings for all the features in the upgraded camera to help you tailor your iPhone 12 Pro camera experience to enable you to get more out of your iPhone.

An Overview of Basic and Advanced Settings

Let's talk about the different camera settings first. Go to the Settings app, and then search for the camera section. After clicking it, a screen will appear in front of you, where you will be able to see different options like Formats, Record video, Record SLO-MO, Record Stereo Sound, Preserve settings, Use Volume up for Burst, Scan QR code, Grid, Mirror front camera, View Outside the Frame, Scene Detection, Prioritize Faster Shooting, Lens correction, and Smart HDR.

Now, to get into the advanced setting for enabling the advanced features, you need to go into the basic ones and then access the further available options like High Efficiency and Most Compatible that are available in Formats, and by default, the camera will have the High Efficiency option on. Higher Efficiency will reduce the size of photos and videos by capturing them in HEIF format, and when sending these files to other devices, you will have to convert them first. My favorite is the Most Compatible as it will capture the photos in JPEG format.

In-depth Review of All the Advance settings

By clicking on the basic settings, you can further explore them. In this section, I will tell you about the things and options you will find when you click on the basic settings.

First is the Format, as I have explained already, where you will find High Efficiency and Most Compatible formats. And you already know, my choice is Most Compatible.

But keep in mind that you will have to enable the High-Efficiency option for 4k 60 fps, 1080p, 240 fps, and HDR videos.

Next will be the Record Video option, and there will be a lot of different formats in which the video can be recorded like:

- 720p at 30 fps
- 1080p at 30 fps
- 1080p at 60 fps
- 4k at 24 fps
- 4k at 30 fps
- 4k at 60 fps

For 4k at 60 fps, as mentioned above, you will have to enable the High-Efficiency option, and if you want to save space, then obviously, you will need to shoot at 720p.

HDR will also require the High-Efficiency mode. Next is the option for Auto FPS and Lock Camera. The Auto FPS will automatically adjust the FPS between 30 to 60 FPS for optimized results.

The Lock camera function is quite interesting because as you shoot a video on an iPhone, it will automatically switch the camera while recording the video. So, by locking it, you can shoot with the camera you want.

In the SLO-MO section, there are three options available, which are as follows:

- 1080p at 120 fps
- 720p at 240 fps
- 1080p at 240 fps (to record at this quality, High-Efficiency mode will be required)

In the Stereo Sound setting, you can enable or disable the stereo sound. The Preserve settings will allow you to preserve the last settings you used in the camera app. With this feature when you open the camera app, it will directly open the mode with the setting you used the last time.

There is also the switch to enable the use of the top button for the burst shot, and by enabling it, you will be able to take burst shots just by pressing the volume up button. Scanning the QR code function will allow the camera to scan the QR codes for all purposes.

The next option is Grid; this is a must turn on option as it will allow you to capture amazing photos. With the help of the Grid, you can place the subject where it suits you better. In short, it will make things easier.

The mirror front camera will allow you to capture the photo, which is not flipped. The View Outside the Frame option will allow you to see extra space outside your camera frame when you click a photo.

The scene detection will help you enhance the photos taken in different backgrounds with intelligent image recognition.

Prioritize Faster Shooting will allow you to capture good quality pictures. This is also related to the device's use of artificial intelligence so that when you press the shutter button fast, this will help you get better quality photos.

Lens Correction, as the name suggests, will remove the distortions and noise in the front-facing and ultra-wide camera.

Smart HDR uses intelligence and mixes the best parts of different exposures in a single photo.

Camera App Settings

Besides the general settings, many other settings can be accessed from within the inbuilt camera app. These settings are available in every mode present in the camera, and you can manually tailor these settings as per your needs and requirements.

For more settings, open the camera app by tapping on it; this will lead you to the photo section of the camera by default. However, if it opens up a different section for you like SLO-MO, Panorama, Video, or Portrait, do not worry and just swipe to the camera section.

There will be an arrow on the top part of the screen; just click it, and it will show you the options available in the photo section. It is highly recommended to set all of these options manually to take the photos to get the best effect.

These options include flash, live photo, night mode, photo size, setting photo exposure, a timer, and lastly filters. There will be a cycle shaped icon at the bottom of the screen in photo mode, which will switch it to the front-facing camera or the selfie camera. The options available for this mode will be the same as in the photo section, and it means the night mode is also available in selfie mode.

In the selfie mode, when you take a picture, it will revert to the right and left in the photo. This means you will get a flipped picture. Some people do not like this. They can therefore choose to enable the mirror function in the settings, or they can also change it through the camera app; after taking a photo, click on edit, then crop it by tapping on the icon in the top left corner.

There are also some zoom options in the photo section that includes; the 0.5 wide-angle, 1-time zoom, or the 2 times optical zoom. Most camera needs can be met with the 2x zoom.

However, if you increase the zoom further, like 4x or 6x, this will take you to digital zoom, and the photo or pixels will become distorted to some extent. You can also just swipe in a circular motion to increase or decrease the zoom. These are all the settings in the photo section. You can click on the arrow at the top again to hide the photo settings section.

After going to the main screen, you can swipe left and see all the modes available on the camera. There is the Time Lapse, SLO-MO, Video, Photo, Portrait, and PANO (Panorama).

Let's discuss the Portrait mode first, as everyone knows, it is a very popular mode and people love to take photos in this mode. There are six panoramic light effects available in this mode to give a professional-looking touch and to enhance the photos.

To utilize these effects swipe in a circular motion on the screen from left to right, and you will be able to switch between different light effects. The effects are Natural Light, Studio Light, Contour Light, Stage Light, Stage Light Mono, and High-Key Mono. And the interesting thing is, these effects are also available in the front-facing camera.

Moreover, different options like flash, night mode, exposure, and timer are also available, but the main difference in this section is the blur control, which is denoted by "f."

Moving on to the next mode, the video mode, which is also a very popular and huge feature in iPhone because there is a lot to it. In the video section, that is not much different from the photo section; in the place of the shutter button, there is the Record button, and for other settings, you have to swipe upwards on the screen.

Here you will be able to see the Flash and Exposure for the video. You can also find the video quality and FPS settings in the top right corner of the screen; you just have to click on the quality and to change them.

SLO-MO is similar to the video mode, just swipe upwards to find flash and exposure settings. On the top right corner are the options to change the quality and frame rate. Next is the Time Lapse. There is not much difference in the settings for it, and the same goes for the Panorama mode.

Tweaking the Settings of the Camera

After getting an overall idea about the different settings related to the camera, we can now proceed to the question of how we can get the most out of the camera or which will be the best settings. Without wasting any more time, let's dive right into it.

If you are new to the iPhone camera or a newbie in iPhone photography, you might feel that it is a bit technical and complex to think about all the difficult stuff about settings.

Most people just go with the default settings as they will simply open the camera, go to the photo and video mode, and click the shutter or record button. They will not bother with the other modes or settings to see what effect those settings will have on the photo. You can just go with the default settings provided to you by the iPhone for the lowest or minimum potential. Still, it is not the recommended way to use the camera because you will miss many interesting things that way.

For the maximum potential, you should use all the different modes present in the camera app. The best mode for taking a sharply focused picture in Portrait mode, because it allows you to select a subject and blur the background.

There are six effects that can be used to get a desired optimum output, so do check them out. Besides, also check the light composition to see if there is a low light condition, then check if the night mode and deep fusion are working or not.

Next, you should also check out the settings menu on the iPhone; you will find two formats their High Efficiency and Most Compatible. For maximum potential, go with Most Compatible. Besides Format, there is also an option named Grid; turn it on, and this will provide a lot of help.

Do not forget to use the ProRAW function, which is only available in iPhone 12 Pro. This feature is so amazing, it allows you to add all the modifications you want to add to your photos when editing.

Make use of the Smart HDR3 and Dolby Vision to produce videos, which are vibrant and full of life.

Enabling Night and Deep Fusion Modes

Two of the main ingredients behind the iPhone 12 Pro success are Night mode and the Deep Fusion mode. So, what is the deep fusion mode, and how can one enable or disable it? Let's talk about it.

Deep fusion is only available in photo mode, and it is utilized automatically by the phone. You do not have to turn it on or off manually. One thing which can stop the deep fusion mode from operating or activating is the "photo capture outside the frame." If this mode is enabled, then deep fusion will not work.

To check this out, go to your settings menu, search for the camera section, and tap on it. Here in the composition section, you will be able to find "photo capture outside the frame." Just turn it off, and you are good to go.

Night mode got a major update in the iPhone 12 Pro, and it is now available for all the cameras, be it rear or front cameras. Like Fusion mode, the Night mode is also available whenever the phone determines that there are low light conditions and Night mode is required.

To check if you can go into the night mode, in the camera app photo section, click on the arrow on top of the screen to see the settings available, normally. The first will be a flash, and next to it is a live photo. Still, when there is low light, the night mode icon will appear between the two settings, and you will be able to see it. When it is available, you can click on it to configure how much assistance you want from the night mode.

Reverting to Original Photo and Video

After capturing a good photo, the last step is always to edit it and give it a finishing touch to enhance the colors, brightness, erase things from the background, or in the case of videos; you might have to trim them down to create the kind of effect you need.

However, after editing, you feel that the photo or video does not look good as you have imagined it would be, or if, for some other reason, you want the original file back, do not worry, for you can always get the original files back very easily.

Just go to the Photos app on the iPhone, click on the photo or video you want to revert to the original, and click on the edit option. Here, you will find a lot of features. Now look at the bottom right corner; you will see the Revert option there; just tap on it and select before the option to revert to the original option. This will remove all the effects that were applied to the photo, and you will get the original file back.

Aspect Ratio and its Uses

The aspect ratio is the dimensions (in terms of width and height) in which a photo is taken. It is an area of composition which is often neglected, but it often plays an important role when taking photos.

You might have noticed that sometimes when you take a photo, there are black bars on either side of the photo, and the photo does not cover all of the screens. This happens due to the difference in the aspect ratio of the screen and photo; for me, this is very irritating, but luckily there is a way to change the aspect ratio of the camera in the iPhone 12 Pro.

Moreover, as the aspect ratio is related to the subject, the frame, and all the space around the subject, the knowledge of aspect ratio will allow you to compose better photos; such knowledge will help you recognize which aspect ratio will look better for the required shot.

To access the aspect ratio, you just have to go to the camera and click on that arrow-like icon at the top of the screen. This will bring up the tool array, and you will find the aspect ratio for the third number. By default, the aspect ratio is set to 4:3, but you can change it to 1:1 square or 16:9 as well.

The aspect ratio can be used to take photos for different platforms; 1:1 can be utilized to take photos for Instagram; similarly, 16:9 provides you a wide-angle look and allow you to capture a wider range of the subject or space within the frame. Another interesting thing is that if you capture a photo in a 16:9 ratio and then realize that you do not like it in that ratio, you can simply crop it to 4:3, and cropping it will not reduce the quality of the photo.

Chapter 7

⌘⌘⌘

A Glance at Using the Camera

Taking a Photo

This chapter will discuss some of the most trailblazing and daunting tips & tricks to take your smartphone photography to the next level.

So, if you are a photography nerd or a beginner and you have spent a heft amount for purchasing the ever classic and Apple's cool new latest iPhone 12 Pro for its camera, you are in here for a treat. Therefore, I would suggest you pay close attention to the details while reading these amazing tips and tricks as you don't need to memorize them, but remembering them while taking a snap can turn your simple forgettable photo into a memorable piece of art.

I am guessing that a lot of people are shocked by the technicalities involved in the act of taking a simple photo with their iPhone. For such people just they wonder why it is not just to click the shutter, and it will be done.

However, let me tell you that photography is a complete art which you are already well aware of because you have the best in your hand. And trust me, with the proper settings, knowledge, and set up, you can create masterpieces with just a simple tick or click in the right direction.

So, open up your iPhone, head to the camera app, and before clicking the shutter to take a photo, here are a few things you should always cover to make your snaps a great deal:

- Control the Exposure
- Do the detailing for a perfect composition
- Use wide and narrow angles
- Never forget to edit & retry

Enlarge Image Q

Once you are done, simply click on the white shutter button on your screen or press any of the volume buttons to capture a photo. Once you are taking the photo, do the necessary tweaking, and as soon as you have got your out of the box image, click just the way you love it.

Taking a Video

In our daily life, be it casual or official, we always felt the need to record a moment. At that moment, we need to have a set of skills and practice that can allow us to use the iPhone 12 Pro effectively for recording.

Apple has made life so easy by enabling us to use Quick Take mode to capture and record videos on a single screen with a slight movement of the, and you just need to know when and how.

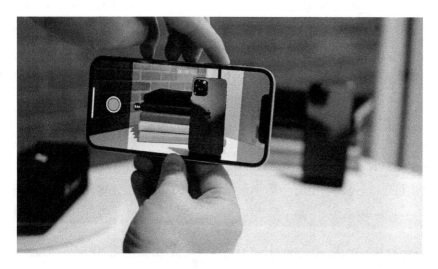

So, if you are witnessing an epic moment or going through your favorite cooking show and cannot afford to forget that part, simply open your iPhone and go to the camera app.

Now, keep that white shutter button or volume button (pressed with your fingers' help), and the recording will start. You will notice it by the shift of the shutter button from white into a red icon. The video will keep on recording until you lift your finger.

Is there another easy and simpler way for it as well? Yes! In here, you can swipe between the modes to reach the video mode, and now by a single tap on the shutter button, you can start the recording until you decide to tap it again to turn it off.

Taking a Portrait Photo

Photography nerds and former iPhone users are aware that portrait mode has been there for a long time now. However, most people are still not used to it and fail to get the maximum from this mode.

On the contrary, Apple is very proud of this amazing feature in their devices, and they have always been keen on improving it. This time around, they have given you a great initiative by enabling iPhone 12 Pro users the liberty to take Portrait photos even at night.

Portrait mode allows the user to capture the studio level clicks by focusing on the chosen object and blurring the rest of the background by using the Depth-of-Field effect.

To take a photo in Portrait mode, swipe right inside the camera app, and once you get to the Portrait mode in the object, you need to focus on it. Once you can line it up, the app itself will start giving you suggestions to get the perfect frame, and by simply following that, you will have the subject in a perfect view in front of you.

Once you have lined it up, you can swipe between the different lighting effects offered to you, like studio light, stage light, or natural light, and others to choose accordingly. Moreover, you can adjust the depth of these light effects by tapping on the depth and light icon shown in front at the top corner to get to the adjustment bar.

Once you are done with all the settings, simply tap the shutter button or a volume key to take the portrait mode snap.

Taking a Panorama Shot

Landscape photography is another amazing feature that comes with the iPhone 12 Pro and if you one who has bought this iPhone 12 Pro for its amazing camera and are fond of taking pictures, you should get to know how to make a perfect panorama shot as this mode of the camera allows us to take 360-degree photos and helps us in covering a much larger area than a normal shot can, even with the use of ultra-wide lenses.

In iPhone, this feature is known as PANO, and you can switch into PANO mode by swiping right in the camera app and take breathtaking shots.

Once you are done with opening the camera and reaching the PANO mode, you simply need to press on the capture and slowly move the camera with the help of your hand or whatever tool you are using to hold the phone in the pointed direction steadily and slowly.

Finally, click on the capture again to complete the shot. After completing all of these steps, it will take a while to compile the photo. There you go! With these simple four to five steps, you have captured a perfect panorama shot.

You can use this amazing feature to capture the mesmerizing landscape views on your visit to a hill station, or you may find it useful in covering the mall you are visiting as it allows you to get all the angles in a single frame. It is something that is fun to try.

Making a Slow-Mo

For photography enthusiasts, Slow Motion video shooting holds great importance as it helps you a great deal in capturing special moments. You can use that mode to a great effect to slowly and steadily capture fast-paced action and at a cinematic effect.

Apple knows it too well and has provided their users an amazing extra feature by introducing the Slow-Mo feature that allows users to capture a series of frames at 60 fps and 1080p, to give users an experience of moving static photos.

You can switch to this mode in the camera app and start capturing it with a simple click; that is not all, you can also toggle into the front Camera now and shoot a "selfie" that also gives you an entertaining and new effect.

Taking a Selfie

Taking a selfie is very easy; if someone asks you to take a selfie, you will just go to the front-facing camera and click the shutter, but you will have to take tons of selfies to find a few or at least one that will be to your liking and this happens with all of us. It happens because taking a good selfie is not that easy, it is a blend of light, angle, filters, and settings.

Taking a Selfie in a Natural Light

The iPhone 12 Pro includes some powerful features to help you in taking excellent selfies. To use the selfie mode, go to the camera app and switch to the front-facing camera.

There will be a small arrow at the top of the screen; you just tap on that arrow to bring up different settings. You will find flash, night mode, aspect ratio, exposure, and timer; setting all of these before taking the photo will help you.

Also, if you are someone like me who is annoyed by the flipping that happens when taking selfies, then there is some good news for you, Apple has introduced the mirror, which allows you to take selfies without the flipping effect. You should also follow some best practices if you want your selfies to be amazing.

Taking a Selfie at Night

As you might already know, it is common sense to take a photo where the light condition is good, and the best light to use for this purpose is the natural light. It can be said that natural light is the best beauty product which is free.

Avoid the shadows at any cost; taking a selfie where a shadow is falling on your face will be the worst thing. It will look like your eyes have dark circles, and your skin tone will also look bad.

Keep trying different angles and make sure to keep your chin down and camera up; this is a very good trick to get some good selfies. Moreover, do not always use the plain camera; you should also try out different filters. There is nothing wrong with editing your photos but make sure not to overdo it. Keep your expressions naturally as they will appeal more and look more genuine to everyone.

Taking a Selfie Video

Some people, especially those who use social media apps, like to take video selfies. I will be telling you some practical tricks which can help you make those selfie videos better.

Go to the front camera, swipe upwards to make use of the options available. You can use flash, set the exposure and quality of the video through these settings.

You can also make use of the Quick Take mode as it allows you to take selfie videos, even when you are taking selfies in the photo mode. To use it, keep pressing the shutter button, and the camera will start recording the video without changing to the video mode.

Try to make the video short, like under one minute, and it will do the magic. When recording, do not look at the screen; instead, look at the camera. This is a very common mistake that people make, they keep looking at their selves when recording the video selfies; when you look at the camera, the people watching it feel like you are talking to them.

Shoot in good light conditions and avoid the shadows instead try to use natural light as much as you can.

The camera should be steady when you are taking a selfie video, and it becomes really hard to keep the hand stable when there is some movement involved. Therefore, use equipment (a gimbal or selfie stick) for this purpose.

Audio is also one of the key factors which can make your video selfies amazing because there should not be any noise. Try not to zoom in, stay natural, express yourself as best as possible, and keep smiling when in front of the camera.

Taking a Live Photo

Even though it looks like a small video, a live photo is just a photo in which the camera starts recording 1.5 seconds before and after you click the shutter button.

To access the live photo function, click on the camera app, make sure you are in the photo mode, and go to the different settings available for this section.

Here you will find the Live Photo mode; by clicking on it, you will see three options available: off, on, and auto. After turning the live photo function on and making the iPhone stable, click the shutter button, and get your live photo. It starts recording 1.5 seconds before and after clicking the function which means that the camera is capturing that whole moment.

In case there is someone who blinked, you do not have to take a new photo; instead, you can go to the edit and click on the small live photo icon; this will allow you to move the keyframe around, and you can choose any moment from the recorded live picture.

Taking a ProRAW Photo

ProRAW feature is recently introduced by Apple, which allows you to capture photos that have some enhancing effects applied to them, but there is still some room for the manual editing you want to do in the photos.

This feature is not enabled by default in the iPhone 12 Pro. To turn it on, go to the settings, click on the camera, then on formats; in the formats section, you will find a toggle that can help you enable or disable the Raw mode.

ProRAW is available on all four cameras present in the iPhone 12 Pro. You will see a RAW button in the camera app to switch immediately from RAW photos to standard images (JPEG).

Use of Focus

When taking a photo, you might find out that the photo is blurry or out of focus; this happens when the subject is not focused properly by the camera.

In iPhone 12 Pro, the camera focuses automatically on the most probable subject in the frame, but you can change that manually. To do that, you just have to tap on the object you want the camera to focus on. When you tap the photo, a yellow square will appear around the object focused by the camera. Moreover, in the iPhone 12 Pro, you can also lock the focus on the particular object, and to do that, tap on the object until "AE/AF Lock" appears on the screen. When this icon appears, it means that the camera is sharply focused on the selected object.

Use of Self-Timer

There are some situations when you are taking a group photo, and you would also want to be in the photo, or when you are alone and want to take your photo in a certain landscape, and there is no to ask help from. At such times, the self-timer option available in the iPhone camera can be a life savior for you.

The timer is available in different modes but generally, go to the camera app, select the photo mode, go to its settings; at the last of those settings, you will find the timer. When you click on the timer icon, you will see three options available; off, 3 seconds, and 10 seconds. You can choose any of them.

Chapter 8

ᏣᏍᎤᏣᏍᎤᏣᏍᎤ

Crafting, Editing, and Configuration

Being a fan of photography and the iPhone are the prerequisites of high demanding individuals. And the era we are living in, with technology and innovation, the expectations have skyrocketed. Now mobile phones are the gadgets that are not only for receiving and making a call; they serve a much bigger purpose than that.

We use our phones for a vast range of activities, be it educational or recreational. Their technology has never failed to amaze us, and in the case of Apple, they have always been a step ahead of the rest. One of Apple's fascinating features in their iPhones was the use of Face ID for unlocking calling and even paying online bills by Apply Pay.

Along with all of these entertaining and amazing innovations, Apple came up with another fantastic feature a few days ago with the introduction of Animoji.

Creation of Animoji and Memoji

Animoji

An Animoji was the same typical emoji with the addition of the ability to recreate and copy the person's expressions using the camera to do the actions and control it. It is amazing and fun for the users as they can mold those typical emoji faces according to their moods. In a way, it gives the freedom of transferring the expressions in a better way. All of these can happen because of the iPhone's awesome camera that can capture your fast-paced expressions and translate them into the perfect Animoji for you to share with friends and family.

Memoji

Jhony Lin, a former Apple employee, is the man behind this awesome, more personalized, and enhanced version of the animoji, called Memoji. A Memoji allows you to create a unique and advanced Animoji having the same type of hairs, eye color, face cut, shape, and much more just as yours to give you a completely familiar-looking digital copy.

Here's how you can create your very own Memoji:

In simple 3 to 4 steps, you can create an outstanding digital Memoji of your own, which will amaze you.

First of all, you have to open your messages app and either click on compose or go to an already existing conversation.

You will see a Memoji button, tap on it, and then swipe right here; you will see another plus sign indicating a new memoji; click on that.

As you have got that memoji of yours, start the customization of hairs, skin tone, eyes, and much more.

Once you are done with the customization, tap on done, and you have created your very own memoji, which you send to anyone you like and innovatively show your expressions.

Sharing a Memoji with a Non-iPhone User

As you have learned how to make an Animoji and then Memoji out of it by simply using built-in apps (which you love using to express your feeling), you may have also noticed that it is an exclusively iPhone built-in messaging app feature. Any Memoji you create is a .mov file that cannot be shared across phone platforms, which means you are not able to share your fun moments with non-iPhone users who use other platforms like android while chatting.

But you don't have to worry, by following the simple steps shown in this book, you will learn how you can create a

GIF out of your saved Memoji and use it on Viber, WhatsApp, and other chatting platforms to share your creations with other users on other platforms as well.

In the first step, enter WhatsApp or any other messaging app you prefer to use and select any contact of your choice. Next, tap on the attachments, then click on + sign and select the video of the Memoji which you want to share.

In the second step, you will see a tap on the upper corner with two options; Video and GIF. Click on the GIF.

In the third step, you just need to press the send button. Your Memoji will automatically get converted into a GIF file that can be shared with your contacts easily.

Third-Party Editing & Capturing Apps

Being a photography lover, you would already have known the importance of editing. Even if you are a beginner, the importance of knowing the use of the best apps to edit and capture the photo is a make or break. But the real dilemma is knowing which apps to choose as there are a plethora of them over the app store, which can be really confusing even for an expert to choose and test all of them.

We have broken them into two parts for you to choose from according to your requirements.

- Photo Editing Apps
- Photo Capturing Apps

Photo Editing Apps

These are the type of apps that will help you edit any photo you have captured. As we all know, a few tweaks here and an ordinary looking photo can be turned into a piece of art that will be the cynosure of all eyes. So, knowing what apps to use to do that little tweaking is really important.

Here is a list of those amazing apps that can help you turn your ordinary photo into a masterpiece:

1. Snapseed
2. VSCO
3. TouchRetouch
4. AfterLight 2
5. Adobe Lightroom CC
6. Lens Distortions
7. Mextures
8. Pixels
9. Superimpose X
10. Enlight

Photo Capturing Apps

Even though the iPhone built-in camera app is state of the art and gives you enough features to take your photography to the pinnacle of fineness, it still won't give you enough control over the camera lenses, especially if you are a DSLR user who likes manual control over iPhone camera and likes adjusting the shutter speed and other things according to your taste. These apps can be a great addition to your photography arsenal.

Here are a few third-party camera apps that will enable you to have that extra control over your iPhone camera:

1. Camera +2
2. ProCamera
3. VSCO App

Accessing Hidden Camera Features

The iPhone camera may seem simple and very easy to use, but there is a lot more to it. So, digging deeper into it can help you a great deal in taking your iPhone photography endeavor to the next level.

We have already gone through a lot of different modes, features, and their uses, but what never fails to amaze me about the iPhone camera is that there is always a bit more to it, which I will discuss here in this section with you to help you take breathtaking photos with your iPhone camera that no one would believe. So, let's dive into something that really sounds kind of crazy, but matters a lot in making you a pro photographer, especially to use the iPhone camera as no one else can.

Open the Camera App in Seconds

The very first feature is a simple horizontal swipe to the left of your phone screen to open the camera app. That might seem very simple and small (like who doesn't know how to open the camera app), but as a photography lover, you may have known that the best photos are those that often last only a few seconds and if we miss the opportunity to capture that, it might never comeback ever.

So, it's really simple and equally critical to know that how to open the iPhone camera in a split of a second so that you could capture those magical clicks that can never be recreated even if we want to do so.

To do that, you simply need to pick up your iPhone, wake it, and quickly swipe your figure from left to right horizontally, and your camera app will open. If in some cases, it fails to happen, you don't need to be worried, simply wake up your iPhone, swipe your finger once from bottom to top, and then repeat the process as already suggested and chances are that you will be able to now use the app this way.

Manual Focus Setup

The second most amazing and hidden technique for taking amazing photos is the setting of focus. It makes a substantial difference in the finishing and detailing of a photo.

If you do not use this focus feature, the iPhone camera will automatically pick the point of focus, and by doing that, you are leaving your snap to chance; sometimes it will turn out to be great, and other times, it won't end up the way you would like; thus, you miss taking control of what you want to capture and leaving your photo at risk.

Doing manual focus is very simple and easy; you just have to tap on the area within your iPhone camera screen. A square box will appear; this will adjust the focus as per the area you have selected, and you will notice how it can change your snaps altogether.

Manual Exposure Setup

This is one of the most outstanding features that make the iPhone stand out, and one that you will ensure if you understand how to use it. It is a professional aspect of photography that can turn a simple photo into a piece of art.

The exposure setting will allow you to manually control the background and foreground light just the way you will love.

Setting the exposure is really simple, all you have to do is place your finger on the screen, and you will immediately notice that while changing the focus, it has automatically changed the exposure as well.

More than just automatically let it choose the settings for you, you can also set the exposure manually by tapping on either the background or the foreground and then swipe your finger up and down to set the exposure value to a value you want and you can start taking great and artistically creative photos that your friends and family will love and admire.

Focus & Exposure Lock

Now that you have learned some of the obvious and hidden features on the iPhone 12 Pro that can help you take artistic photos, you will need to keep practicing a bit more in order to keep on taking those amazing photos without much of a hassle. Locking your Focus and Exposure is one of such features.

This locking feature can help you a great deal in doing that. The focus and exposure you have set have been reported to sometimes change accidentally, or the iPhone reverting to the normal setting once you are done snapping a photo.

If, however, you want to keep on taking photos using a previous setting you have made, you will need the same focus and exposure to remain intact, and the use of this locking feature can do that.

So, to lock the focus & exposure, what you need to do is put your finger in the middle of the screen and hold it for two to three seconds until you see an AE/AF Lock appearing on the screen.

You can now set the exposure accordingly, and it will remain that way, no matter what happens on the scene or how many photos you take.

Click Photos with Volume Button

If you are a photographer and also an iPhone photographer who loves capturing photos via DSLR or any other professional camera, you will find this feature really amazing as you know that you can get used to the physical shutter button it becomes easy to capture the photo.

It can be difficult to adjust to the on-screen shutter, but nothing to worry about because this cool feature, which enables you to use the volume buttons as a shutter, will make your life really easy and will give you that same kind of feeling you get when using a professional camera.

Its use is very simple and easy; you don't need to do any configuration for that as the iPhone 12 Pro has this feature enabled as a built-in feature. All you have to do is frame a photo and press either of these volume buttons to capture a perfect photo.

Capturing Photos with Apple's Hands-free

This is the last, though not the least-hidden technique that I am going to share with you to help you out in crafting the best photos ever.

This amazing technique can surpass all other in two ways, and it is my favorite as well; first of all, it allows you to do candid photography along with perfectly unnoticed portraits, and secondly, this technique is really useful while taking a photo with a tripod and especially when you don't want your iPhone to get disturbed.

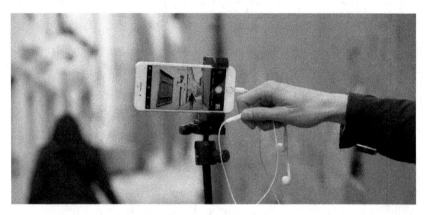

To do this, simply plug in your headphone and use either of the volume buttons present on the headphone to release the shutter. By using this simple and cool technique, you can take amazing and perfectly framed photos.

Conclusion

Apple has allowed us to glimpse the future; it wants us to adapt to these changes ahead of time as these features will become available very soon.

This phone is for people who love photography and like to create content on social media platforms and for people who want to stay competitive on Instagram, TikTok, Facebook, and all other platforms.

Those also in the field of filmographies who want to create videos that are full of life and vigor, with the help of Dolby Vision to give a professional and inspirational touch to their video will find the iPhone 12 Pro very useful to them.

This phone is also for the people who are very social and love to visit places with low light, parties, and bars and in short, for all the people who love nightlife to enjoy pictures with the help of a reinforced night mode system. It is also for those people who enjoy interactive AR technology. The AR technology in iPhone 12 Pro is very advanced due to the LiDAR sensor.

I hope you make the best of your iPhone 12 Pro camera.

SPECIAL BONUS!
Get this additional Book of Taking Better Selfies with the iPhone
100% FREE!

Hundreds of others are already enjoying insider access to all of my current and future books 100% free!

If you want insider access plus this Taking Better Selfies with the iPhone, all you have to do is **scan the code** below with a QR Reader on your smartphone camera or device to claim your offer!

www.ingramcontent.com/pod-product-compliance
Lightning Source LLC
LaVergne TN
LVHW051246050326
832903LV00028B/2605